# NEW WAY

# Lion is ill
## and
# The Greedy Guzzler

Hannie Truijens

D1329142

Nelson

# Lion is ill

I am ill, said Lion.

Who will bring me food.

Fox was sorry for Lion.

I will, he said.

I am very ill, said Lion.

Who will bring me food.

Monkey was sorry for Lion.

I will, she said.

Oh I am very ill, said Lion.

Who will bring me food.

Rabbit was sorry for Lion.

I will, he said.

Oh oh I am so ill,

said Lion.

Who will bring me food.

Mole was sorry for Lion.

I will, she said.

Oh oh I am so very ill,
said Lion.
Who will bring me food.
Rat was sorry for Lion.
I will, he said.

Rat went to Lion with food.

He looked down.

Oh dear, he said.

They were very silly.

Fox, Monkey, Rabbit and Mole
went to Lion.
But they didn't come back.
Lion ate them all up.

I won't help you Lion,
said Rat.
You are better now.
And I am not that silly.

# The Greedy Guzzler

I want my food.

**I WANT MY FOOD.**

**I WANT MY FOOD,**

said the Greedy Guzzler.

I will eat a little fish,
said the Greedy Guzzler,
with a pot full of chips.
So he did.

I will eat two hens, said

the Greedy Guzzler,

with two egg sandwiches.

So he did.

I will eat a little pig,

said the Greedy Guzzler,

with an apple.

So he did.

I will eat some buns, said
the Greedy Guzzler,
with red jam.
So he did.

I will eat two ice creams,

said the Greedy Guzzler.

So he did.

Now I am full, he said.

I am so full, said the Greedy
Guzzler, that I will POP.
And he did.